FRENCH CULINARY ART

ALAIN MARTIN

Copyright © 2017 by Alain Martin. All Right Reserved.

No part of this publication may be reproduced, distributed, or transmitted in any form or by any means, including photocopying, recording, or other electronic or mechanical methods, or by any information storage and retrieval system without the prior written permission of the publisher, except in the case of very brief quotations embodied in critical reviews and certain other noncommercial uses permitted by copyright law.

ISBN-13: 978-1981539130
ISBN-10: 1981539131

CONTENTS

3   **№ 1**   FRENCH CUISINE

5   **№ 2**   WHY DON'T THE FRENCH GAIN WEIGHT?

7   **№ 3**   COLD APPETIZERS HORS-D'ŒUVRE FROIDS

23   **№ 4**   WARM APPETIZERS – HORS-D'ŒUVRE CHAUDS

31   **№ 5**   SOUPS - LES POTAGES

FISH AND SEAFOOD № 6	37
MEAT AND GAME LA VIANDE № 7	45
MEATLESS MEALS № 8	61
DESSERTS - LE DÉSERT № 9	73
FRENCH GASTRONOMY № 10	101

ABBREVIATIONS AND UNIT CONVERSIONS

1 cup = about 250 ml of liquids
4 cups = about 1 liter
The base unit is the cup, the derivative (smaller) units are tablesppon (abb. **tbsp**) and teaspoon (abb. **tsp**).
1 cup = 8 fluid ounce = 2,365882365 dl;
1 tbsp = 1/16 cup = 1,478 cl, 1tsp = 1/3 tbsp = 0,498 cl

1 g = 1 gram = 0,001 kilograms
1 l = 1 liter = 1 000 mililitres (ml)
125 ml = about 8 spoons = ½ cup
1 tablespoon = 1 leveled tbsp = 10 – 20 g* = 15 ml (of liquids)
1 teaspoon = 1 leveled tsp = 3 – 7 g* = 5 ml (of liquids)

*The weight of one cup or one spoon of a dry ingredient greatly varies, based on their density, ie: a cup of flour has a lower weight than a cup of butter.

The values of dry ingredients are applied to the ingredients mentioned in the text, directly following the value, such as 1 spoon of chopped onions or ½ cup of grated cheese.

In some cases, the text contains a number of ingredients in grams, as well as spoons or cups, which may fasten the procedures.

Where applicable, the amount is rounded up or down.

N°1 FRENCH CUISINE

Every country adores its football stars, movie actors or rock legends. For the French, these are sided by yet another category: the top chefs, thanks to whom the fame of French cuisine spread across the globe.

The best chefs continually discover new, refined, highly regarded and admired combinations of tastes. New talents follow their footsteps and race in ingenuity, so that they too may become recognized and respected experts.

Gastronomic guides and various culinary-themed publications annually reward a number of stars, chef's caps and points to a staggering number of restaurants. Like this, you may choose famous restaurants, new talents or try out local specialities and enjoy traditional meals, such as French onion soup, incredible „cassoulet" from the region of Toulouse, „choucroute" – Alsatian sauerkraut recipe, „potée auvergnate" – the pot from Auvergne, declared fish speciality – „bouillabaisse", and others. A talented chef can be found by his enthusiasm for the choice of high-quality ingredients and his care for the use of local products.

For the French, food is much more than just nutrition for the body. Cooking in France became a culinary dialogue, that encompasses history, philosophy, and art. Cooking and sharing of food is an act of delight, a privileged moment when the French spend time together and enjoy the talk.

Cooking and cuisine are considered as an art, in France. It is a part of French identity. French cuisine is diverse and includes a wide spectrum of types of cooking, including, what is known as molecular gastronomy and makes use of science to transform tastes and scents in the meal. This, however, doesn't mean that cooking is turning into a science: on its own, it's still art.

„Good morning", a French couple says, gives each other a kiss and seat themselves for breakfast. Still, there are some, those just eat up some „café-crème" white coffee with croissants, on their way to work. Once there, they have a couple more coffees, before heading to company's canteen.

French lunch, even in this kind of canteen, consists of several courses, in a free flow. Other than meat with salad, loads of raw vegetables, at any season, are served as appetizers. All accompanied by a French baguette.

Daily, after the main course, the dessert is served, either fresh or compote fruit, dairy products (puddings, creams or yogurts), or alternatively fruit cakes and ice creams.

The cherry-on-the-top of every meal is coffee.

The French cuisine may be described by many adjectives. It is healthy, fragrant, sophisticated, inspiring and delicious. France benefits from its ideal location. Coastal areas offer seafood, the highlands yield cheeses of the highest quality, the plains feature aromatic wines. The gastronomy of neighboring states enriches the borderlands, such as regions of Alsace, Basque, Country or Corsica. The main basis of French cuisine is quality and first-class ingredients. The French have a well-developed sense of taste and smell and they are the champions in combining spices and ingredients. The French leave very little, from the well mad food, which they enjoy almost every time, on their plate. At home or in the common restaurants, once the meal is over, the remaining sauce is wiped by a piece of BAGUETTE.

Across France, the wine is served with the food, that is grown in almost all the regions, with the exception of the north. Wine and cheese are the main protagonists of French cuisine. However, this varies with seasons of the year. In the summer, it is packed with all sorts of fruits and vegetables, mushrooms take the stage at the end of the summer, the hunting season and therefore the season of game meat lasts between September and February, the season of oysters culminates in winter. Herbs are irreplaceable: tarragon, rosemary, marjoram, lavender, thyme, fennel, sage, ...even regardless of the season of the year. They are often tied into 'bouquet garni', the bunch of herbs, that doesn't have a steady composition. It is thrown into the meal just before the end of the preparation and is taken out before serving.

The rich literature of the French cuisine hints its diversity and almost ‚scientifically' exact preparation. The classic recipes, nature of the preparation and other culinary tips are encompassed in the „Larousse de la cuisine française" lexicon, that is essentially the Sacred Scripture of the art. Many competitions in preparing various meals or desserts are held and the French are willing to spend hours in the kitchen, just to impress and amaze their guests.

The most famous chefs of Paris:
Alain Ducasse, Guy Savoy, Pierre Gagnaire, Alain Sanderens.
The most famous chefs outside of Paris:
Blanc of Vonnas, Bernard Loiseau of Saulieu, Paul Bocuse of Lyon, Marc Veyrat of Annecy, Pourcel of Montpellier.

France is known for its gastronomy, that has been included in the UNESCO Representative List of the Intangible Cultural Heritage of Humanity.

No 2

WHY DON'T THE FRENCH GAIN WEIGHT?

Although the French aren't ranked among the first in obesity rankings, the people of France aren't obsessed with healthy eating, yet the right diet is widely available. However, if the French really care about something, it is their lunch, eaten at a given time and, if possible, with the family.

It is important, for the French family, that all its members sit around the table at a given time and enjoy a common meal. That's why things such as going into the fridge during the day or eating whatever and whenever you like aren't common in France.

About a half of the population eats their lunch at half past twelve or at one pm and eating large portions of food or small snacks in between the main meals aren't common French features.

How do the French eat?

...they enjoy the food with all their senses. They think of good food without feeling guilty about it.

...they eat at least three times a day, often treating themselves to multiple courses. However, they load smaller portions and more importantly, they eat more fruits, vegetables, and yogurts, commonly treating themselves to a nice bowl of soup in the evening.

...they don't eat a lot of bread. For breakfast, they enjoy a cup of coffee or a fresh orange squash but, more importantly, they do it with taste and pleasure.

...they drink a lot of water and many herbal teas. A bottle of mineral water or a carafe of tap water is always found at the table, during the meal. Regardless, they like to treat themselves to a bottle of delicious wine for lunch.

...they enjoy their meal at a well-spread table. They don't eat in front of the TV or on the go.

...they don't count their calories and they surely don't weight themselves every single day. Instead of getting crazy about their weight, they build on the nice and pleasant feelings.

When their trousers get too tight, they become more aware of their food but avoid radical diets.

.... they don't forbid themselves from anything and they treat themselves to little rewards. Always in the reasonable amounts, they like to enjoy a quality dark chocolate.

.... they are no fitness fanatics, but they care about plenty of movement. They often walk to work or take the stairs over the elevator.

.... they care about the quality and variety of their groceries. They cook from fresh and seasonal ingredients and don't buy finished or semi-finished meals. An endless spectrum of herbs and spices is used to season their dishes.

Bon appétit!

Nº 3

COLD APPETIZERS
HORS-D'ŒUVRE FROIDS

Meat pastes, hams, seafood, stuffed fruits or vegetables are some of the appetizers served. The main course tends to be fish or meat, with a sauce and a side dish. Generally, it can be said, that the cuisine is among the healthiest in the world, thanks to the low-fat contents, large amounts of fruits and vegetables and low sugar levels of the dishes.

The order of meals of the French cuisine became the template for other European cuisines.

In the French cuisine, appetizers are served as the first meal instead of or just before the soup. Most of them can be served independently. They are made from various types of meat, eggs, salads, butter spreads, cheese, fish, smoked products etc. These ingredients are also used to make or decorate sandwiches, canapes, meat pastes etc.

BEETROOT IN SALT CRUST - BETTERAVE EN CROÛTE DE SEL

INGREDIENTS:

3 raw beetroots
1 ½ kg salt
olive oil
balsamic cream
black grounded pepper
chive

MAKES 4 SERVINGS

PREPARATION:

Wash and dry the beetroots. Don't peel it. Cover the bottom of a bowl with a thick layer of salt. Place the beetroot into the bowl and cover it with salt.

Bake it in a preheated oven at 160°C (320°F), for 1 ½ hours.

Let it cool for about 30 minutes, clean the beetroot thoroughly and peel the skin.

Chop the beetroot into thin slices, like carpaccio. Season with black grounded pepper, sprinkle it with chopped chive and decorate the plate with balsamic cream.

EGGS FLORENTINE – ŒUFS Á LA FLORENTINE

INGREDIENTS:

4 eggs
1 shallot
125 ml (½ cup) white wine
125 ml (½ cup) cream
125 ml (½ cup) wine vinegar
300 g spinach
4 slices of a very thin hard cheese
100 g (½ cup) butter
salt, pepper, nutmeg

MAKES 4 SERVINGS

PREPARATION:

Chop the shallot in half and cut it into thick slices. Melt a spoon of butter in the pot and add the shallot. Once the shallot caramelized, pour the chicken bouillon (or water) and white wine. Braise it and add the cream. Reduce it and move it to the blender. Add 50g (1/4 cup) of butter and mix it, until a soft cream is formed.

Boil water. Add salt and wine vinegar. Carefully place eggs and boil for 5 minutes. Afterward, take the eggs out and place them into cold water. Peel carefully.

Take a spinach leaf and cut a circle with a diameter 1 cm. Keep it for decorations. Place the spinach into boiling water and blanch it for about 2 minutes. Then take them out and cool them quickly in icy water. Remove and drain the water, by placing it in a sifter. Mix into a purée.

Use the cheese to cut out two circles for every egg, with diameters of about 2 cm. In the middle of a circle, cut out a smaller circle with a diameter of about 1 cm. Place the blended spinach on the plate. Place the circle of cheese, with the hole in the middle. Place the circle of spinach on top of the egg and cover it with the circle of cheese. Slightly burn the cheese. Pour the shallot sauce over it.

EGGS IN MEURETTE - ŒUF EN MEURETTE

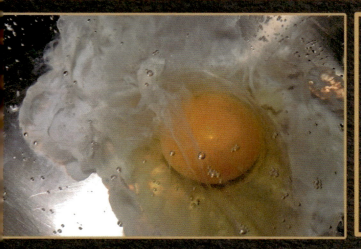

INGREDIENTS:

- 4 extra fresh eggs
- egg white from one egg
- 1 onion
- 250 g (2 cups) mushrooms
- 150 g (1 cup) bacon
- 100 g (½ cup) butter
- 4 slices of bread
- 2 dl (1 cup) red wine
- 0,5 l (2 ½ cup) calf broth
- 1 tbsp vinegar
- 1 bunch of parsley

MAKES 4 SERVINGS

PREPARATION:

Pour water into a pot and add a spoon of salt and a tablespoon of vinegar. Smash an egg into a mug, such that yolk remains compact and add a little vinegar. Boil the water and create a vortex, by stirring it with a wooden spoon. Carefully pour the egg into the boiling and the swirling water and boil it for 2 ½ to 3 minutes. Remove the egg and place it onto an absorbing paper. Cut the unnecessary projections, so that the egg looks nice and smooth.

Chop the bacon, onion, and mushrooms into small cubes. Melt and slather the butter, add bacon, onion, and mushrooms. Roast.

Steadily add wine and continue roasting. Pour the broth and reduce by a half.

Cut the crust of the bread and place in between two baking papers. Sheet the bread into a thin layer, using a roller. Cut a circle and cover it with the egg white. Chop the parsley leaves and press the bread into it, so that as much parsley attaches to the bread. Bake at 170°C (338°F), between two baking papers. Load it with a pot of water, so that the bread doesn't deform. After a while, remove the pot and remove the upper paper. Once the bread is dry enough, remove it from the oven.

Roast the onion on the butter, until it turns brown. Caramelize slightly. Cut the mushrooms into thin slices. Place the egg into the mix with mushrooms and heat slightly.

Serve the mushroom mix, egg in the middle and baked parsley bread on top. Decorate with caramelized onion and mushroom chips.

SMOKED SALMON WITH GOAT CHEESE - SAUMON FUME AU FROMAGE

INGREDIENTS:

For smoked salmon
100 g of smoked salmon

For Goat Cheese Cream and Mustard
60 g of goat cheese
3 tsp old-style mustard
1 tsp of Dijon mustard
1 tsp of cider vinegar

For old-fashioned mustard vinaigrette
5 tbsp of sunflower oil
3 tsp old-style mustard
1 tsp of Dijon mustard
1 tsp of cider vinegar
Pepper and salt

For garnish
10 cherry tomatoes
5 young onions
1 apple

MAKES 4 SERVINGS

PREPARATION:

For smoked salmon
100 g of smoked salmon
Sliced the smoked salmon and set aside.

For Goat Cheese Cream and Old Fashioned Mustard
60 g of goat cheese
3 teaspoons old-style mustard
1 teaspoon of Dijon mustard
1 teaspoon of cider vinegar

Pepper
In a bowl, combine goat's cheese, both mustard and vinegar. Pepper and reserve.

For old-fashioned mustard vinaigrette
5 tablespoons of sunflower oil
3 teaspoons old-style mustard
1 teaspoon of Dijon mustard
1 teaspoon of cider vinegar
Pepper and salt
In a bowl, mix the sunflower oil with the two types of mustard and cider vinegar. Pepper, salt and reserve.

For garnish
10 cherry tomatoes, 5 young onions, 1 apple
Slice the cherry tomatoes and reserve in a bowl. Then finely slice the onions and set aside. Cut out the julienne apple and again, book.

For dressage
Smoked Salmon. Goat's cheese with old-fashioned mustard Old-fashioned mustard vinaigrette The filling (cherry tomatoes, young onions and apple) Two beautiful cressonnette handles Arrange the smoked salmon on a plate. Add the goat cheese in small slices. Gently place the garnish and season with the salad dressing. Decorate with cress and serve!

FIFTY SHADES OF PARIS - LES CINQUANTE NUANCES DE PARIS

INGREDIENTS:

14 large brown mushrooms
2 white mushrooms
1 dl (½ cup) double cream
parsley leaves

MAKES 4 SERVINGS

PREPARATION:

Remove the stems of the brown mushroom (3 heads per person). Put the heads of the brown mushrooms into a pan, with no oil or fat. Bake at a low temperature, head down. Bake until the heads are filled with the mushroom liquid. Add 2 thinly sliced brown mushrooms and similarly, roast them without fat.

Mix the stems of the brown mushrooms and add white mushrooms chopped into cubes. Roast the mix and pour into the cream. When it starts boiling, take it off the flame, blend it and let it cool. Serve by pouring the blended mix and placing the heads on top, sprinkling by roasted mushroom plates. Lastly, decorate with parsley.

FRENCH STYLE STUFFED EGGS - OEUFS MIMOSA

INGREDIENTS:

2 eggs
1 tbsp mayonnaise
salt, grounded black pepper

MAKES 4 SERVINGS

PREPARATION:

Put the eggs into cold water and boil. When the water begins to boil, keep the eggs boiling for 10 more minutes. Afterward, cool and peel them.

Split the eggs into two halves.

Put three yolks along with a spoon of mayonnaise into the bowl. Add salt and pepper and mix into a cream. Fill 4 egg halves with the cream.

Put a half of a yolk into the colander and push through, right onto the eggs. Place the eggs into the fridge and serve chilled.

CEVICHE FROM ST. JAMES SHELLS WITH FRESH CORIANDER AND CHILI PEPPERS

INGREDIENTS:

4 St. James shells
2 young onions
2 radishes
1 lemon
leaves of coriander
2 tbsp olive oil
chilli peppers

MAKES 4 SERVINGS

PREPARATION:

Firstly, rinse leaves of coriander and put them into the water, to preserve freshness.

Preparation of the St. James shells:

Firstly, you must cut the vein of the shell. Prepare the lemon juice, crush it entirely to let give out more juice. Cut it and squash the juice, of which plenty should be ready so that shells may be cooked well and the food may be good. Season with some chili peppers, not much of salt and some grounded black pepper. Add lemon juice.

Cut the radish into quarters and then further halve every piece. Chop the onion into the smallest possible pieces. Cut everything once more. Add to the shells. Add two additional spoons of lemon juice and the same amount of oil. Cool in the fridge.

№4

WARM APPETIZERS – HORS-D'ŒUVRE CHAUDS

Warm appetizers are a so-called warm by-course, as they are served in small portions, at a point between the serving of soup and main course. Most commonly, they are made from eggs, vegetables, fish, and rice. The most common warm appetizers, those are even prepared in our homes, such as Eggs Florentine, different risottos, ragouts and others.

Other than above mentioned warm appetizers, the French cuisine also knows many more foods, served as warm by-course, of those we choose the most interesting ones.

BAKERY WITH ASPARAGUS AND HERB BUTTER

INGREDIENTS:

40 pieces of green asparagus
100 g (½ cup) butter
100 ml (½ cup) crème fraîche or sour cream
4 – 5 stems of chervil or coriander
250 g puff pastry
flour
sea salt
salt, grounded black pepper

MAKES 4 SERVINGS

Fresh asparagus must be processed as soon as possible since it dries quickly. If it can't be processed immediately after the purchase, it is storable in the fridge, in the vegetable tray, packed in a moist cloth, for two to three days.

PREPARATION:

Gently peel the asparagus under the small heads and its scaly leaves, using a small knife. (Be wary of the green tissues, so that the knife does not damage them.)

Cut the bottom part of the shoots using the scraper. Carefully wash and dry the asparagus.

At the floured kitchen desk, cut the puff pastry to form the rectangles 11 x 7 cm. Slices of dough are placed on the baking tin, placed inside the oven at 200°C (390°F), baking them for 15 – 20 minutes. Meanwhile, boil asparagus for 15 minutes in salty water.

Chervil or coriander will be cut into big bits. Asparagus is taken out of the water and left in a warm place. Reduce the water from asparagus by evaporating, then add the crème fraîche and sour cream and season according to your taste. Add butter and stir the chopped chervil or coriander into the mix, by bits.

Halve the baked slices of puff pastry. Re-heat asparagus and shorten to about 15 cm, it should be longer than the puff pastry. Cut asparagus ends are sliced into small pieces.

Place on a plate, fill with a fill with asparagus cubes and cover them with a few long springs. Cover them with the upper half of the dough and decorate the surroundings with chervil sauce.

SIRLOIN SKEWER

INGREDIENTS:

Meat
200 g sirloin
1 tbsp oil

Roquefort sauce:
100 g Roquefort
2 dl (1 cup) white wine
2 stems of chive
1 dl (½ cup) crème fraîche or sour cream

Shallot sauce:
1 shallot
1 tbsp cane sugar
2 dl (1 cup) red wine
1 stem thyme
1 dl (½ cup) demi-glace (or broth)

MAKES 4 SERVINGS

PREPARATION:

Two sauces will be prepared. One will be based on Roquefort, the base of the other is shallot.

Roquefort sauce:
Cut the Roquefort and place it in the pot. Heat steadily until it melts. Pour in the white wine and cook at a mild flame for about 10 minutes. Once the wine reduced, add crème fraîche or sour cream and cook on, for a while. Let it cool and sprinkle with chive.

Shallot sauce:
Let the butter melt in a smaller saucepan. Add shallot, cut into circles and pot roast over a mild flame, until the shallot turns brown and starts to caramelize. Help the caramelisation process by adding a tablespoon of cane sugar. Stir and braise for 10 minutes, on a smaller flame. Once shallots are brown and soft, add the red wine and demi-glace (or broth). Season with salt and pepper and to make the taste more dominant, add some thyme. Strengthen the flame and reduce the sauce, until it becomes more viscous.

Slice the meat, following the fibers (sideways), so that the skewers look better. Cut the meat until they for thin noodles and then cut again to form a square and rectangular pieces.

Pour some oil onto the pan and roast the skewers from all sides, but pay attention to avoid overdoing the meat on the inside.

Roast for 3 – 4 minutes. 5 at most.

Remove the skewers and let the meat rest for about 5 min. Serve with both sauces.

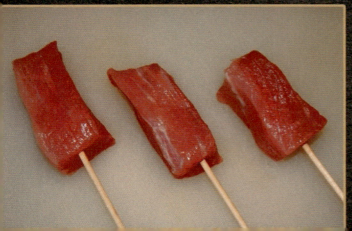

HAM WITH BEETROOT

INGREDIENTS:

2 kg smoked ham
1 kg beetroot
50 g (¼ cup) fresh horseradish
½ tsp cumin
50 ml (¼ cup) vinegar
1 tsp salt
150 g (¾ cup) sugar

MAKES 4 SERVINGS

PREPARATION:

Firstly, weight the ham, because the length of cooking depends on the ham's weight. A rule applies, stating that the meat must be cooked for the same amount of time, as is its weight, but of course, there are exceptions to the rule. For example, 1,5 kg smoked loin or the neck will be cooked for 1 ½ hours, but 1 kg of rolled shoulder must be cooked for more than one hour since it is tougher than the neck. 1,5 kg of rolled smoked shoulder ought to be cooked for over 2 hours, also depending on the meat quality. If the meat is covered in a net, ease it off the meat, but don't remove it. Otherwise, when the meat expands the net might get stuck in the meat and during the removal, we would also remove chunks of meat. Place the smoked ham into the boiling water, wait until it starts boiling again and boils on for 2 – 3 minutes – 5 minutes for larger pieces and hams with bone.

By this short cooking the meat ‚contracts' and keeps the juices inside. After the five minutes, lower the temperature lower the temperature to 80 – 85 degrees and keep it steady until the end of the process. After it is done, leave the meat in the water to cool. Pull the net and cut with a sharp knife. The ham should be nicely colored and juicy.

Shred the boiled and cleaned beetroot, to form fine slices, put them into a large pot, add fresh grated horseradish and cumin. Stir thoroughly. Create the dressing by mixing water, vinegar, salt and 50 g of sugar and pouring it to cover the beetroot. Don't pour all of it. Let it rest for 2 – 4 hours and then serve. Use the pan to form a caramel. Caramelize 100 g of sugar and add circular slices of ham. Roast on both sides and place it in a mold. Cover the ham with beetroot and horseradish. Decorate with parsley leaves and cubes of jelly, made from beetroot juice.

5 SOUPS - LES POTAGES

Soups – the fundamental element of French soups is the broth of bones or beef, which is then variously enriched and amended by garnish and ingredients. In France, soups are usually served at dinner time, as the second meal, right after appetizers, or as the first course, if the appetizers aren't served. They are to be served warm on pre-prepared hot plates. A liter of soup tends to be distributed between 4 diners. They are made from different quality ingredients. Often they are differently strong broths – consommé, bouillons, those are often strengthened with minced meat and purified with egg whites. White soups are made from vegetables, namely peas, asparagus, leek, meat, fish, poultry, such as ragout, but may also include potatoes, mushrooms etc. Onion soup is one of the most popular ones, is made from roasted onion cooked in beef broth, baked with chopped toasts and grated cheese. St. Germain, Crème Dubarry or Consommé Colbert, Julienne are some of the soups listed in menus of the renowned world hotels. Cold fruit soups are also popular, especially in the summer months and are often served as refreshing snacks.

ONION SOUP

INGREDIENTS:

6 larger onions
sea salt
spices (thyme, bay leaf, black whole pepper, colourful pepper),
5 tbsp sunflower oil
1 liter (4 cups) dry white wine
1 liter (4 cups) chicken broth
250 g gruyere cheese
1 baguette

MAKES 4 SERVINGS

PREPARATION:

Peel, halve the onions and slice to get rings. Heat a large pan, pour in the sunflower oil and add the onion rings. Roast them coverless on a very weak flame, until it softens wholly. Don't add the salt just yet. This last for 15 – 20 minutes. Cover and braise for about 10 minutes. Stir and pour in the liter of wine. Uncover the pan and let all of the wine evaporate. Season with salt and pepper, and lastly pour in the broth. Cover again and cook for some 20 min.

Cut the baguette to get thin slices. Bake in the oven at about 200° C (390° F) for some 10 minutes, in order for them to dry. Then put the slices of baguette into the bowl. Draw the soup into a bowl and sift with large amounts of gruyere cheese. Bake it in the oven for 10 minutes. Serve hot.

BOUILABAISSE

INGREDIENTS:

ROUILLE
One 3-inch piece of baguette, cut into 1/2-inch dice
3 tbsp water
2 garlic cloves
1/2 tsp cayenne pepper
1/2 tsp kosher salt
3 tbsp extra-virgin olive oil

BOUILLABAISSE
3 tbsp extra-virgin olive oil, plus more for drizzling
2 leeks, white and light green parts only, thinly sliced
1 onion, cut into 1/4-inch dice
1 fennel bulb - fronds reserved, bulb cored and cut into 1/4-inch dice
4 garlic cloves, 3 coarsely chopped
2 tomatoes, cut into 1/2-inch dice
2 bay leaves
Pinch of saffron threads
2 tbsp pastis or Pernod
5 cups store-bought fish stock
One 2-pound live lobster
Eight 1/2-inch-thick baguette slices, cut on the bias
3 Yukon Gold potatoes, peeled and cut into 1/2-inch dice
1/4 tsp cayenne pepper
2 dozen littleneck clams, scrubbed
1 pound monkfish, cut into sixteen 1 1/2-inch pieces
1 pound skinless red snapper fillets, cut into sixteen 1 1/2-inch pieces
1 pound skinless halibut fillet, cut into sixteen 1 1/2-inch pieces

MAKES 4 SERVINGS

PREPARATION:

In a mini food processor, sprinkle the diced bread with the water and let stand until the water is absorbed, about 5 minutes. Add the garlic, cayenne and salt and process until the bread and garlic are coarsely chopped. With the machine on, drizzle in the olive oil and process until the rouille is smooth. Transfer to a bowl and refrigerate.

In a very large, deep skillet, heat the 3 tablespoons of olive oil. Add the leeks, onion, fennel and chopped garlic and cook over moderate heat until translucent, about 5 minutes. Add the tomatoes and cook until they begin to break down, about 5 minutes. Add the bay leaves, saffron and pastis and bring to a boil. Add the fish stock and bring to a simmer. Cook over low heat until the vegetables are very tender, about 20 minutes. Discard the bay leaves.

In a food processor, pulse the vegetables and broth to a coarse puree. Strain through a fine sieve set over the skillet.

Bring a large pot of water to a boil. Add the lobster and cook until it turns bright red, about 4 minutes. Drain and rinse the lobster under cold water until cool enough to handle. Remove the tail, claw and knuckle meat and cut into 1-inch pieces.

Preheat the broiler. Arrange the baguette slices on a baking sheet and broil them 6 inches from the heat for about 1 minute per side, until the slices are golden brown around the edges. Rub each slice with the remaining whole garlic clove and drizzle lightly with olive oil.

Add the potatoes and cayenne pepper to the broth and bring to a simmer. Cook over moderately high heat until the potatoes are just tender, about 10 minutes; season with salt and pepper. Add the clams, cover and cook over moderate heat until they just begin to open, about 3 minutes. Add the monkfish, cover and simmer for 2 minutes. Add the lobster, snapper and halibut, cover and simmer until the clams are open and all the fish is cooked through, about 4 minutes.

Set a baguette toast in each of 8 shallow bowls. Ladle the fish and broth over the toasts and top each serving with 1 tablespoon of the rouille. Sprinkle with fennel fronds and serve immediately.

№ 6

FISH AND SEAFOOD

The closer you are to the sea in France, the more olive oil, fish and vegetables you'll find. The French adore the Mediterranean cuisine and frequently prepare sea creatures for dinner. For example, mussels of St. James are very popular. Bridade de morue, a dish from cod, is very popular too, along with anchovies, regardless if they're fresh or pickled.

Les fruits de mer – seafood – are a separate category in French menus. That wouldn't be too odd, as France is a coastal country, but instead, the odd feature is the method of preparation in each region. With lemon and salted butter, or filled and dried..., seafood is a sought-after specialty, especially in regions closer to the Atlantic.

SAUMON CONFIT À BASSE TEMPERATURE

INGREDIENTS:

4 salmon fillets with skin
1 liter (4 cups) olive oil
1 lemon
1 orange
2 tsp coriander
4 twigs of thyme
1 clove of garlic
1 cucumber

MAKES 4 SERVINGS

Before preparation, let the fish adjust to room temperature.

PREPARATION:

Throw coriander, shred lemon and orange peel into a pan. Add the clove of garlic and some thyme. Roast. Pour a liter of olive oil and heat up. Let it cool.

Heat up a spoon of oil and swiftly roast the salmon. Add some salt to the fish. Move it to the plate and remove the roasted skin.

Roast the skin separately, until it isn't well done. To assure that it remains straight throughout the roasting process, load it with another smaller pan. Cut squares out of it and place aside. It will be used to decorate.

Place the salmon into an oil filled pan and put it in an oven, pre-heated to 60°C (140°F). Confit for 20 min.

Peel the cucumber and slice it to form very thin slices. Add salt and put aside for some 30 minutes.

Cut circles or balls of the cucumber. Heat up the oil, add the cucumbers, finely chopped garlic and a pinch of salt. Bake for 1 – 2 minutes.

Decorate with orange, lemon, and a cucumber. Serve.

ROASTED SALMON WITH AN ORANGE SAUCE

INGREDIENTS:

800 g fresh salmon
sea salt
grounded black pepper
olive oil
2 oranges
1 tsp finely chopped ginger
1 tbsp sugar cane
2 tbsp butter
1 kg potatoes
1 onion

MAKES 4 SERVINGS

PREPARATION:

Remove the scales from the washed and tided salmon. Season with salt and black pepper. Roast the salmon on a hot pan, with a little of the olive oil, initially skin down. We can press it with the turner, so that the skin roasts evenly.

Meanwhile, prepare the orange segments. Cut out the bark and divide the skinless orange into crescent-like segments. Place them into a bowl and squash the juice of the remaining oranges to the orange crescents.

Once the salmon skin gets crunchy, turn it and add the ginger and sugar cane. Once sugar caramelizes, add the orange segments and juice. Cook over a mild flame. Lastly, add butter and wait until it melts.

Potato pancakes:

Grate washed potatoes and garlic on a fine shredder. Move to the sifter and let it rinse. Heat the olive oil in a pan. Place the potato dough onto a pan using a spoon, forming smaller pancakes. Roast on both sides, until they turn gold/brown.

SIEVED FISH IN DUTCH SAUCE

INGREDIENTS:

4 pieces of fish fillet (turbot, cod)	**Dutch sauce:**
500 g potatoes	200 g (14 tbsp) butter
100 ml (7 tbsp) milk	3 yolks
2 lemons	juice of ½ of a lemon
1 bunch of parsley leaves	pinch of cayenne spices
sea salt	salt

MAKES 4 SERVINGS

PREPARATION:

Peel the potatoes. Cut them, using a small knife, such that all have an approximately the same size. Cook in salty water.

Using a big knife, get the fillet rid of the skin. Wash, dry and take the meat aside.

If you want to get the sauce right, be very careful. Melt the butter in the saucepan and remove the whey. In the water bath, whisk the yolks with 3 spoons of water, so that a smooth cream forms. Once the sauce is too viscous, dilute it with some cold water.

Remove the saucepan from the water bath and add the heated butter by drops, during continual stirring. Season with a pinch of salt and cayenne spices. Lastly, add the lemon juice. Cover the completed Dutch sauce and place into a warm environment, but not a warm water bath, as it could curdle at a temperature as low as 65°C (150°F).

Pour a liter (4 cups) of cold water into a sufficiently large saucepan, so that the fillets may fit into it. Add milk and season with a pinch of sea salt.

Put the fish fillets into the saucepan with milk, let it boil and maintain the weak boiling state for 5 minutes. Afterward, drain the fish and serve it on a plate with potatoes. Pour the sauce over it, at last.

Decorate with parsley leaves and lemon.

№7

MEAT AND GAME
LA VIANDE

The main course – Le repas principal – is the meat (la viande). Game, poultry, pork (to a lesser extent), rabbits, sheepmeat as well as beef...in the form of steaks, commonly lightly roasted, bloody or medium. It is served with vegetable garnish, dips and tasted kinds of butter...

VOLAILLE FERMIÈRE, PURÉE DE POMMES DE TERRE

INGREDIENTS:

2 chicken breasts with wings
100 g (½ cup) butter
250 g (1 cup) chicken broth
500 g (2 cups) milk
50 g (¼ cup) cream
50 g (½ cup) almonds
500 g potatoes
150 g (¾ cup) dry white wine
1 egg
salt, pepper, olive oil

MAKES 4 SERVINGS

PREPARATION:

Cut the chicken wing along with the breasts. Cut the chicken hull to small pieces.

Peel and cut the potatoes to get cubes. Pour a milk into a saucepan and add the potatoes. Add the salt and boil it covered. Roast the almonds on the pan, until it goes gold and add about a quarter into the milk with potatoes.

Season the chicken breasts with salt and pepper. Heat the butter with olive oil on the pan and roast the breasts, skin down. Don't turn the breasts. If the skin is done to the golden tune, move the breast to the oven, pre-heated to 230°C (440°F) and bake for about 7 minutes, skin up.

Rinse the potatoes through the sifter, add the cream and a spoon of butter. Stir into a mash with a smooth consistency. Add a ¼ of the almonds and the egg yolk. Heat the mash with the yolk over the water bath, so that the yolk doesn't remain raw.

Remove the fat from the pan, where you baked the breasts and insert the cut chicken hull. Add ¼ of the almonds, pour in the milk, that was rinsed from the potatoes, add the white wine too and lastly pour in the chicken broth. Cook for about 10 minutes to reduce the liquid. Rinse through the sifter.

Cut the breasts into four parts, cover with the liquid and sprinkle with remaining almonds. Serve with green salad and the mashed potatoes.

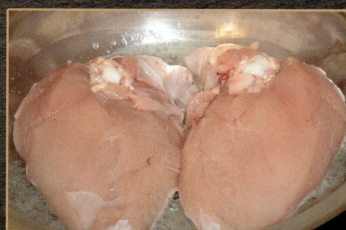

COCK ON WINE - COQ AU VIN

INGREDIENTS:

- 4 bone-in, skin-on chicken thighs
- 1 pinch kosher salt and freshly ground black pepper to taste
- 1 cup bacon, sliced crosswise into 1/2-inch pieces
- 10 large button mushrooms, quartered
- 1/2 large yellow onion, diced
- 2 shallots, sliced
- 2 teaspoons all-purpose flour
- 2 teaspoons butter
- 1 1/2 cups red wine
- 6 sprigs fresh thyme
- 1 cup chicken broth

MAKES 4 SERVINGS

PREPARATION:

Preheat oven to 190°C (375°F).

Season chicken thighs all over with salt and black pepper.

Place bacon in a large, oven-proof skillet and cook over medium-high heat, turning occasionally, until evenly browned, about 10 minutes. Transfer bacon with a slotted spoon to a paper-towel lined plate, leaving drippings in the skillet.

Increase heat to high and place chicken, skin-side down, into skillet. Cook in hot skillet until browned, 2 to 4 minutes per side. Transfer chicken to a plate; drain and discard all but 1 tablespoon drippings from the skillet.

Lower heat to medium-high; saute mushrooms, onion, and shallots with a pinch of salt in the hot skillet until golden and caramelized, 7 to 12 minutes.

Stir flour and butter into vegetable mixture until completely incorporated, about 1 minute.

Pour red wine into the skillet and bring to a boil while scraping browned bits of food off of the bottom of the pan with a wooden spoon. Stir bacon and thyme into red wine mixture; simmer until wine is about 1/3 reduced, 3 to 5 minutes. Pour chicken broth into wine mixture and set chicken thighs into skillet; bring wine and stock to a simmer.

Cook chicken in the preheated oven for 30 minutes. Spoon pan juices over the chicken and continue cooking until no longer pink at the bone and the juices run clear, about 30 minutes more.

An instant-read thermometer inserted into the thickest part of the thigh, near the bone should read 74°C (165°F). Transfer chicken to a platter.

Place skillet over high heat and reduce pan juices, skimming fat off the top as necessary, until sauce thickens slightly, about 5 minutes. Season with salt and pepper; remove and discard thyme. Pour sauce over chicken.

LA POULARDE DE BRESSE – BRESSE CHICKEN

INGREDIENTS:

1 chicken (2kg)
1 onion
2 cloves of garlic
100 g (1 cup) brown mushrooms
1 tbsp flour
150 ml (¾ cup) wine Champagne
1 l (4 cups) cream
60 g (¼ cup) puree of foie gras
100 g (½ cup) butter
salt and black grounded pepper
1 twig of thyme

MAKES 4 SERVINGS

PREPARATION:

Portion the chicken by removing the thighs and dividing each into two parts. The breasts, wings, and hull remain in one piece. Salt and rub the hull with butter. Bake at 180°C (350°F) in a pre-heated oven, for 15 – 20 minutes.

Heat 2 spoons of butter in a pan and fry the chicken thighs, skin down. Salt and pepper, add thyme. If the skin is done, turn the thighs, add finely cut onions, mushrooms and 2 cloves of garlic, cut into small pieces. If the mix caramelized, sprinkle with flour and pour in the champagne.

Occasionally stir it, while cooking over a mild flame. If the mix is reduced, add cream and cook for some 30 minutes.

Remove the thighs and percolate the sauce. Add the puree from foie gras into the sauce and pour in 2 spoons of champagne. Mix it together. Portion the grilled breasts, add the baked thighs and suffuse it all with the sauce.

Cut the mushrooms into slices and roast on butter, until golden/brown. Add salt and pepper. Also, fry the peeled and whole garlic cloves on butter.

Serve the chicken with the sauce, place the fried mushrooms and roasted garlic cloves on top.

BACON-WRAPPED PORK TENDERLOIN WITH SOUR CHERRY SAUCE

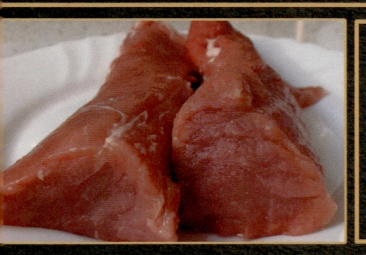

INGREDIENTS:

1 pork tenderloin
Kosher salt and freshly ground pepper
400 g bacon slices
1 tsp olive oil
8 shallots, halved
1/2 cup dried sour cherries
3/4 cup chicken stock
1 tsp cornstarch
Chopped fresh dill, for garnish, optional

MAKES 4 SERVINGS

PREPARATION:

Preheat the oven to 200°C (400°F). Pat dry the pork tenderloin and sprinkle with 1/2 teaspoon salt and 1/2 teaspoon pepper, then wrap with the bacon, overlapping the slices.

Heat the oil in a large nonstick skillet over medium high heat until hot, then brown the pork and shallots, 6 to 8 minutes. Flip the pork tenderloin browned-side up and transfer the skillet to the oven. Roast until the pork reaches 60°C (145°F) in the center, 15 to 18 minutes.

When the pork is done, transfer to a cutting board, leaving the shallots in the skillet. Add the cherries and stock to the skillet and bring to a simmer. Stir together the cornstarch and 1 tablespoon water, then add to the skillet, bring to a boil, whisking until sauce is thickened, about 2 minutes. Season the sauce with salt and pepper. Slice the pork into 8 pieces, divide among 4 plates with the sauce, and sprinkle with dill, if desired.

LE FILET MIGNON DE PORC

INGREDIENTS:

1 sirloin	¼ cup bacon
2 carrots	2 apples
2 onions	2 pears
1 garlic	½ celery
1 shallot	½ orange
1 liter (4 cups) milk	salted butter
1 anchovy 1 pineapple	salt and pepper

MAKES 4 SERVINGS

PREPARATION:

Boil the milk in a pot.

In the second pot: cut the carrot diagonally and then slice bigger circular pieces askew. Chop the shallot to get larger cubes. Place it in the pan. Add a clove of garlic. The pan must be cold. Add a pinch of salt. Steadily stir and heat the vegetables. Add a spoon of butter and slices of bacon. Steam shortly. Season the filet mignon with salt and pepper. Add it to the steamed vegetables and continue to stew it together. Pour the boiling milk into the mix. Cook slowly for 7 – 12 minutes at 95°C (200°F). Once cooked, remove the filet mignon and let it rest.

Boil water in the third pot, add a pinch of salt and place sliced celery triangles into the bath. Cook until soft, remove from the water and place to cold water bath, to eliminate further cooking.

Cut crescents of apple and pear, along with its peels and remove the seeds. Extract circles of pineapple and cut them into quarters. Roast apples and pears on a pan with a spoon of butter. Add celery and continue to roast the mix. On a separate pan, brace the pineapple on butter and the juice from half of an orange.

Add the roasted apples, pears and celery to the pineapple pot and cook it covered, so that a nice layer of glaze forms.

Quickly fry the filet mignon on butter, so that it gets nice brownish edges. Remove and slice askew. Serve with glazed fruits.

ROASTED GRAPE BACON WRAPPED FILET MIGNON

INGREDIENTS:

3 cups red grapes
4 Grass Fed Filet Mignon
10 strips of bacon
4 tbsp balsamic vinegar
2 tbsp olive oil
pinch of salt

MAKES 4 SERVINGS

PREPARATION:

Preheat oven to 200°C (400°F). Place a piece of parchment paper in an 8x12 glass baking dish (for easy clean up, but no big deal if you don't have any).

Throw your grapes, balsamic vinegar, and olive oil with a bit of salt on top into your baking dish and toss to coat. Roast grapes for about 25 minutes or until soft. When there is about 10 minutes left for your grapes to cook, pull out a medium skillet and place over medium heat.

While your skillet heats up, wrap your bacon around the outer rim of your filet mignon. Use a toothpick to press through part of the meat to connect your bacon ends. Don't want that bacon sneak away from your meat!

Salt both sides of your filet mignon, just a little bit. Now first place your bacon sides onto your hot skillet to release some of the fat to cook the meat on.

Cook bacon on all sides for about a minute each side, then place your filet mignon into the bacon fat and cook for around 4-5 minutes per side (this time will depend on how thick your filet mignon is and how you prefer yours cooked. mine was cooked to medium rare).

Top filet mignon with roasted grapes and a bit of the leftover balsamic vinegar that is reserved in the baking dish.

PORK CHOPS PREPARED ON WHITE WINE WITH GRATIN POTATOES

INGREDIENTS:

4 - 6 pork chops
1 onion
1 kg potatoes
250 ml (1 cup) white wine
50 g (¼ cup) butter
salt and grounded black pepper
6 bacon slices

MAKES 4 SERVINGS

PREPARATION:

Peel, wash and cut the potatoes or slice to three mm thick slices. Tenderize the chops. Salt and pepper them. Cut onion to get thin circles.

Grease the baking bowl with butter, lay the first layer of potatoes and salt it. It is crucial to salt every layer of potatoes individually. Form another layer of the pork chops and cover it with onion rings. Then continue to create more layers of potatoes, meat, and onions. The last layer should be a layer of potatoes, those are to be covered with bacon slices. Suffuse in white wine.

Bake for 1 hour, at a temperature of 180°C (360°F). Before finishing the baking, place a piece of butter on top of the potatoes.

№8 MEATLESS MEALS

This category includes the courses, those don't contain any meats. Meatless meals contribute to the balance of nutrients in the organism and diversify the menus. They tend to be energetically and biologically valuable and easily digestible

Types: vegetable, cereals, pasta, potatoes, rice, cheese, legumes, mushrooms, eggs and others.

GRATIN DAUPHINOIS – GRATINE POTATOES

INGREDIENTS:

1,5 kg potatoes
2 cloves of garlic
250 dl (1 cup) cream
100 g (½ cup) butter
1 liter (4 cups) milk
nutmeg
salt

MAKES 6 SERVINGS

PREPARATION:

Wash and cut peeled potatoes, to get thin slices (remark: if the potatoes are cut don't wash them any further, the starch is needed for the right consistency).

Cook milk in a pot, add crushed garlic, salt, and nutmeg, then the potatoes. Keep them submerged in milk and boil for 10 – 15 minutes, over a mild flame.

Preheat the oven to 180°C (350°F). Grease the baking bowl with butter and move the potatoes into the bowl. Pour over with cream and place a piece of butter on top. Put it into the oven and bake for 50 minutes, until the potatoes will be golden on the surface.

RATATOUILLE

INGREDIENTS:

2 zucchinis
2 eggplants
6 tomatoes
1 onion
2 carrots
2 celery stems
30 g (1 tbsp) butter
30 ml (1 tbsp) olive oil,
1 tsp garlic
500 g (2 cups) tomato puree
3 twigs of fresh thyme
salt, grounded black pepper,
6 fresh basil leaves

MAKES 4 SERVINGS

PREPARATION:

Make a small cross into the peel of the tomatoes, boil enough water and once boiled, place the tomatoes into the water for 1 minute, at most. Take them out quickly and put them into the cold water now. Peel and cut them to thin wheels. Do the same with the eggplant and the zucchinis, salt them from both sides and dry, using a napkin.

Wash the carrot, peel and cut. Cut celery and onions to get small pieces. Melt a piece of butter on the pan with olive oil, fry the carrot, celery and onions. Season with salt and crushed garlic. Add tomato puree and stew it. Blend the mix together with basil leaves. Fill the bottom of the baking bowl with the blend and gradually place the vegetable wheels on top.

Depending on the shape of the baking bowl, cut out baking paper, cover the bowl and bake in the oven, which is preheated to 200°C (390°F), for 45 minutes. Then remove the paper and bake for 10 extra minutes.

MUSHROOM CUPCAKES

INGREDIENTS:

500 g puff pastry
250 g mushrooms
1 onion
150 g bacon
100 g (½ tbsp) butter
2 dl (1 cup) red wine
1 egg

MAKES 4 SERVINGS

PREPARATION:

Roll the puff pastry, until it is thin. By using a cutter cut larger circles. Rub the muffin mold with butter, so that the dough doesn't stick to the mold. Place a circle into the mold and press it with a cup, so that a cupcake is formed.

Prepare the filling. Cut the bacon, onion, and mushrooms to get cubes. Melt and foam the butter, add bacon, onion, and mushrooms. Fry.

Steadily pour the wine in and continue to fry. It should have a viscous consistency. Fill the cupcakes with the filling.

Use a smaller cutter to cut out smaller circles and cover them with butter and use them to cover cupcakes.

Rub with the yolk and pierce with a fork, so that the air can escape. Bake at 180°C (350°F), for 10 – 15 minutes, until it's goldish/brown.

FILLED BAKED POTATOES

INGREDIENTS:

8 potatoes
100 g bacon
200 g ham
250 g mushrooms
100 g hard cheese
1 onions
50 g (¼ cup) butter
salt

MAKES 4 SERVINGS

PREPARATION:

Wash and boil potatoes until soft. Then halve them into a pan and hollow them out, so that the sides are still thick enough.

Fry onions with mushrooms in butter and bacon. Cut the ham into fine, small pieces, shred the cheese and let the onion and mushrooms cool. Salt the potatoes and mash them.

Mix it together and carefully fill the hollow potatoes with the blend. Place in a preheated oven for 10 minutes. If your potatoes weren't cooked enough, keep them in the oven for longer. Decorate with baked ham.

BAKED CHEESE "FONDUE"

INGREDIENTS:

2 boxes soft cheese camembert
2 garlic cloves, sliced
1 sprig rosemary, leaves picked
1 pinch chilli flakes
few slices truffle

MAKES 4 SERVINGS

PREPARATION:

For the baked cheese 'fondue', preheat the oven to 180°C (350°F).

Remove all the packaging from one of the cheeses and place it back in the box. Place the lid under the base for extra support. Score the top of the cheese in a lattice pattern.

Using a spoon, push the crushed garlic, rosemary and chilli flakes into one of the cheeses. Push the truffle slices into the other cheese.

Place onto a baking tray and bake in the oven for about 30 minutes, or until the cheese starts to go wobbly in the middle.

Remove from the oven and allow to rest for five minutes.

N°9 DESSERTS - LE DÉSERT

French desserts are admired across the globe. Its creations are attractive, delicious and they bring moments when we hope that the moment lasts forever. French Boulangerie-pâtisserie, which translates into bakery-patisserie, are inseparably bonded with France.

They are symbols of Sunday meals, family feasts or long evenings, multiple courses of which are topped with the pastries or cakes. The joy of minutes of walk to the nearest patisserie, the choosing of the pastry, the short chat with the vendor and the feeling of carrying the paper box, tied with a cord, filled with the delicious delights enjoyed by every Frenchman.

VANILLA PANCAKES

INGREDIENTS:

4 whole eggs
250 g (2 cups) flour
500 ml (2 cups) milk
125 g (½ cups) sugar
180 g (¾ cup) butter
salt, vanilla pods
1 tbsp olive oil
2 tbsp brown sugar
candied orange peel
1 orange
1 tbsp orange liqueur

MAKES 4 SERVINGS

PREPARATION:

Fry the butter for 8 – 10 minutes, until the water evaporates.

Whisk eggs with sugar. When the dough is mixed, add a pinc of salt and continue to whish it. Add the flour and stir until the dough remains smooth.

Heat, don't boil, milk in the pan, with a spoon of olive oil and a vanilla pod. Pour in the molten butter, mix and heat for 2 minutes. Continually pour the mix into the dough and continue to stir. Once the dough is smooth, strain it through the sifter and store it in the fridge for 2 hours.

Prepare very thin pancakes from this dough. Fold to a quarter.

Melt a spoon of butter and add brown sugar. Once the sugar begins to caramelize, add the juice of an orange and candied orange peel. Reduce it and add 2 pancakes. Add a drop of alcohol and flame it. Add two additional pancakes, cook for two minutes and serve.

May be served with vanilla ice cream.

ROASTED PINEAPPLE

MAKES 4 SERVINGS

PREPARATION:

INGREDIENTS:

For roasting the Pineapple
1 large Pineapple
150g (½ cup) Vanilla syrup
200g (¾ cup) Caster sugar
2 Lime
1 Lemon
1 Orange
10 leaves Mint

For the caramel sauce
200g (¾ cup) sugar
50g (¼ cup) Unsalted butter
200ml (¾ cup) Water
25ml (2 tbsp) Rum

Ingredients for the dried pineapple slices
8 slices Pineapple
1/4 Lemon juiced
100ml (½ cup) Water
1tbsp Caster sugar

Ingredients for the Pineapple sorbet
750g Pineapple flesh, sweet, large. Peeled, cored and cut into 1cm pieces
110g (½ cup) Caster sugar
1/2 Lime, juiced

For roasting the Pineapple
Preheat the oven to 170°C (340°F). Slice 8 rounds of pineapple from the base no thicker than 1mm and reserve for the dried pineapple slices. Brush the prepared pineapple in the vanilla syrup and roll in the citrus sugar. Place upright in a small frying pan and roast in the oven for 2 hours basting with half of the caramel sauce every 15 minutes (see below). To finish mix the chopped mint in the remaining citrus sugar and roll the roasted pineapple in this and leave to cool slightly before carving.

For the caramel sauce
In a small sautepan on a medium heat, melt the caster sugar and cook to a golden caramel. De-glaze with the butter and trimmings from the pineapple, add the water, cognac and bring to the boil. Simmer for 10 min. After the pineapple has been roasting for 15 minutes ladle over half of the caramel sauce and continue to baste every 15 minutes.

Drying the pineapple slices
Pre-heat the oven to the 100°C (210°F). Place the reserved slices of pineapple into a bowl and squeeze over the lemon juice. In a small pan bring the water and sugar to a boil and pour over the pineapple slices. Leave until they have cooled. Drain the syrup from the pineapple slices and place then next to one another on the two non-stick trays. Place both trays in the pre-heated oven and dry slowly for 45 minutes to 1 hour until the pineapples have dried completely. Check occasionally to make sure they do not darken.

Remove the trays from the oven and whilst still hot, use a palette knife to slide the pineapple slices off the trays, leave to cool, place in an airtight container cover and reserve.

Making the Pineapple sorbet
Macerate all the ingredients together for 30 minutes. Puree in a blender and churn in an icecream machine. Reserve in the freezer until needed.

To serve
Cut the pineapple in half and portion in 8 equal pieces. Place to the left of the plate and garnish with the sorbet, dried slices and scatter around the cherries (if you are using) and any remaining citrus sugar.

MARINATED PINEAPPLE

INGREDIENTS:

½ Pineapple
Lemon sorbet, ready-made (a scoop)

For syrup
500 ml (2 cups) Water
250g (1 cup) Sugar
30g (¼ cup) Ginger
2 Limes
Forgarnish Berries (optional)

Pomegranate seeds (optional)
Mint leaves (optional)

Pineapplecooked at lowtemperature
½ Pineapple cleaned and choppedintopieces
1 tbsp butter
2 tbsp rum
1 tbsp brown sugar
1 vanilla

MAKES 4 SERVINGS

PREPARATION:

Prepare the pineapple
Remove the pineapple skin, but leave the "eyes" visible to avoid wasting flesh. Using the tip of a knife, scoop out the eyes one at a time.

Slice the pineapple
Use a meat slicer (preferably), mandolin or knife to cut the pineapple into paper-thin slices. The slices should be slightly translucent and, if using a knife, the blade should be visible through the pineapple.

Make the syrup
In a small pot, boil the water, sugar, ginger and zest of two limes.

Arrange
In a deep dish or container, pour the hot syrup over the pineapple slices.

Refrigerate
Cover with cling wrap and refrigerate for at least 24 hours.

Pineapple cooked at low temperature, infused and aromatised
Place the chopped pineapple in a small vacuum bag with the rum, butter, sugar and vanilla and leave to cook for 40 minutes at 70°C (160°F).

Once chilled, store until ready to serve.

PINEAPPLE CARPACCIO WITH POMEGRANATE

INGREDIENTS:

1 large ripe pineapple
1 pomegranate
leaves Small bunch of mint shredded

FOR THE VANILLA SALT
125 g (½ cup) sea salt or fleur de sel
1 vanilla pod split open and seeds scraped out

MAKES 4 SERVINGS

PREPARATION:

First make the vanilla salt. Put the salt and vanilla seeds into a bowl and mix well. Place in an airtight container with the empty pod and use as required in baking or savoury dishes. The mixture will keep indefinitely.

Cut off the ends of the pineapple, then slice off the skin from top to bottom, keeping the fruit whole. Cut the pineapple widthways into slices about 1mm thick so you end up with lots of circles. Set aside.

Cut the pomegranate in half horizontally. Hold each half in turn over a bowl and smack the skin with the back of a wooden spoon so that the seeds drop into the bowl. Reserve any juice that comes out of the seeds as you remove them.

To serve, sprinkle a serving platter with a little vanilla salt. Arrange the pineapple slices over it, then sprinkle with a little extra vanilla salt, the pomegranate seeds and juice. Finish with a light sprinkling of the vanilla salt and the shredded mint leaves.

USING SALT IN SWEET DISHES
Adding a little salt to sweet dishes actually enhances the sweetness. I often add a pinch to cakes, biscuits and especially caramel sauces. Vanilla salt would work well in all of these, too. Try it also sprinkled over a buttery fillet of white fish.

RASPBERRY - ALMOND TART

INGREDIENTS:

300 g (1 ¼ cup) raspberries
biscuits
white chocolate
1 vanilla pod
1 lemon
500 ml (2 cups) whipped cream
mint leaves
125 g (½ cup) sugar
125 g (½ cup) grated almonds
2 eggs
2 tbsp butter
1 tbsp flour

MAKES 4 SERVINGS

PREPARATION:

Crush white chocolate (only a handful) and melt it in a pot, so that the chocolate turns liquid. Add vanilla and lemon peels. Add crushed biscuits (about 3 pieces) into the dough, take aside and stir.

Pour the dough into a circular mold, about 5 cm wide and press, until it remains about 1 cm thick. Then remove the form. Shape the wheels and put into the freezer for 5 minutes, for the dough to thicken.

Meanwhile, put a spoon of sugar on to a pan, when it begins to go brown and 1/3 of the raspberries and cook. Strain through the sifter and let the syrup cool.

Prepare the almond hat by mixing almonds, sugar, seeds from the vanilla pod and 2 egg whites. Melt butter and pour into the mix. Stir it together and let it cool.

Add flour and mix again. Place a circular mold on to the baking paper or the silicon foil and pour the mix into it. Fix with the fork, so that the mix is evenly spread in the mold. Bake at 180°C (360°F), for 10 minutes. They should catch a nice golden color.

Cover the biscuit base with whipping cream, pour over with the raspberry syrup and decorate with raspberries and mint leaves. Leave the almond hat on the side.

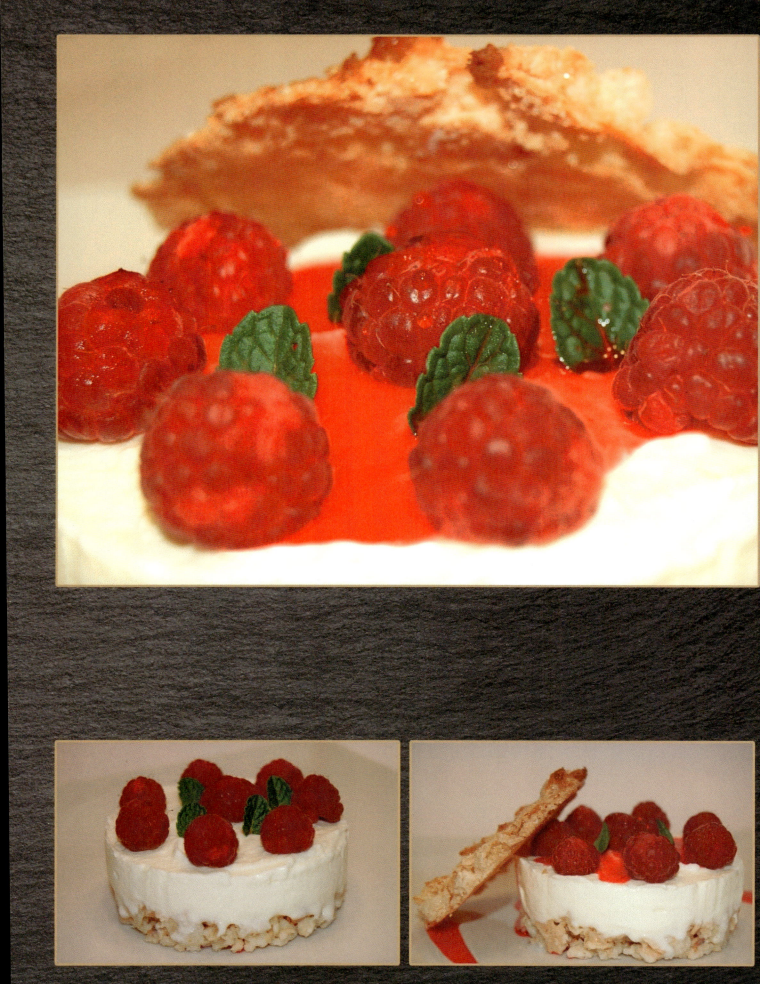

STRAWBERRY TART WITH GOLDEN HAIRS

INGREDIENTS:
4 eggs
4 tbsp semi-thick flour
4 tbsp sugar powder
1 vanilla sugar
1/3 of a pack of baking soda
butter and flour to grease the mold
1 kg (4 cups) fresh strawberries
strawberry jam
500 ml (2 cups) whipping cream
2 cups sugar, ½ cup water

MAKES 8 SERVINGS

PREPARATION:

Firstly, prepare the tart mold and preheat the oven to 200°C (390°F). Separate the egg whites from the yolks into two separate bowls. Whisk the egg whites, sugar and vanilla sugar to get the beaten egg white - snow.

Slowly add the yolks to the snow. Once the yolks are well included in the snow, lightly mix the flour in with the baking soda. Pour the stuff into the mold and put it into the oven. Bake for 15 – 20 minutes.

After baking the dough, let it cool and whisk whipping cream from a cream. In meantime, wash the strawberries and let them dry on a paper towel.

Once the cake has cooled, take it out of the form and cut into three pieces. Spread strawberry jam on the bottom one, in the amount that you see fit and cover with the second layer. Halve the strawberries and lay them on the tarte. Place a layer of halved strawberries and add the whipping cream. Cover with the third layer of tarte and sprinkle with sugar powder.

Put two cups of sugar and ½ cup of water into a pot. Boil while stirring continually over a mild flame. Once molten, cover and boil for 2 – 3 minutes, then uncover it and boil until it reaches a temperature of 310°C (590°F), with occasional stirring. The caramel must have a golden cover and can't be burnt. Shut the flame, take aside and place it into a prepared larger pot of cold water for some 2 – 3 minutes, until it gets runny. WARNING: manipulations with warm caramel might be slightly dangerous.

Soak a fork in the caramel and quickly run it, which forms the caramel golden hair. Decorate the tarts to your liking with strawberries and caramel hairs.

STRAWBERRY WITH VANILLA CREAM

INGREDIENTS:

200 ml (¾ cup) milk
200 ml (¾ cup) whipping cream
1/2 tbsp gelatin powder
1/4 cup sugar
1 tsp vanilla extract
Strawberry Sauce
450 g (2 cup) fresh strawberries
2 tbsp water
70 g (¼ cup) sugar

MAKES 4 SERVINGS

PREPARATION:

Dissolve gelatin in 2 tbsp cold water and let it swell for about 5 to 10 minutes.

In a medium saucepan bring the cream, milk and sugar to a simmer over medium-low heat (Do not boil). When sugar has dissolved remove from heat and add vanilla extract. Let cool for 5 minutes before adding the gelatin.

Add gelatin in the milk mixture and stir until the gelatin has completely dissolved. Pour it in the serving glasses (I've used 5 oz - 150 ml capacity glasses) or ramekins and refrigerate until it sets, for about 4 hrs or better overnight.

To prepare the sauce wash the strawberries, drain well and remove leaves. Cut strawberries in quarters.

In a small saucepan put the strawberries, sugar and water. Bring to a simmer and remove from heat immediately.

Pour into the bowl of a blender or food processor and blend the mixture to make a smooth sauce. Pass through a strainer to remove the seeds out of the sauce. Cover and let it cool to room temperature then refrigerate until ready to serve.

Before serving pour the strawberry sauce over the vanilla cream and serve.

STRAWBERRY BITES WITH BALSAMICO-CARAMEL CREAM

INGREDIENTS:

250 g (2 cups) strawberries
3 tbsp sugar
1 dl (½ cup) red wine
1 tbsp balsamic vinegar
basil

MAKES 4 SERVINGS

PREPARATION:

Put three spoons of sugar into the pan. Pour the red wine in, but just so much to cover the sugar. Add a tablespoon of balsamic vinegar. Mix and reduce, to get a thick stuff.

Halve the strawberries.

Cut the basil into thin noodles and sprinkle the strawberries with it.

PEAR CUPCAKES IN CARAMEL

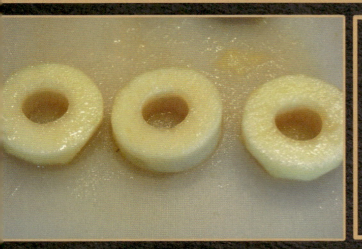

INGREDIENTS:

4 pears
50 g (¼ cup) butter
90 g (½ cup) brown sugar
500 g puff pastry
1 egg

MAKES 4 SERVINGS

PREPARATION:

Roll the puff pastry to get a thin plate. Cut out larger wheels using a cutter. Grease the cupcake mold with butter, so to avoid the sticking of the pastry to the mold. Cover the mold with the wheels and press with a cup, to create a cupcake.

Peel the pear and using a knife cut few wheels. Use a small cutter to remove the midsection of the pear. Place the wheel on the cupcake.

Heat up 30 g (2 tbsp) of butter and 90 g (1/2 cup) of cane sugar. Once the sugar begins to caramelize, put it into the cupcakes by pouring over the pear.

Use a smaller cutter to cut out smaller wheels of the puff pastry. Lubricate them with a yolk and pierce with a fork, so that the air might escape. Bake at 200°C (390°F), for about 10 – 15 minutes, until it turns golden in color.

Once baked carefully tilt the cupcakes out of the molds.

PEARS ON PUFF PASTRY

INGREDIENTS:

250 g puff pastry
2 tbsp sugar powder
1 egg
4 pears

MAKES 4 SERVINGS

PREPARATION:

Cut the puff pastry to get squares. Peel the pears and cut out circles. Lay pear wheels on to the baking paper and grease up with butter. Place them on top of the puff pastry squares. Pierce with a fork, to create room for the escaping of the steam and cover with yolk.

Heat the oven to 180°C (350°C) and bake until golden in color.

Take them out of the oven, turn and sprinkle with sugar powder.

LA TARTE TATIN

INGREDIENTS:

8 large apples
600 g (3 cups) sugar
500 g (2 cups) butter
500 ml (2 cups) water
2 pieces of vanilla
250 g puff pastry
apricot jam

MAKES 4 SERVINGS

PREPARATION:

100 g (1/2 cup) of sugar is needed to prepare the caramel. Put 1/3 of the sugar into a dry pan and heat at a mid-ranged temperature. Once the sugar is fully liquified add the second third of the sugar etc. Stir slightly, so that the sugar doesn't burn. Once caramelized, pour the sugar evenly into a mold and let it cool.

Peel the apples, slice to get cloves and remove the seeds.

Put 500g (2 cups) of cubes of butter, 500 g (2 ½ cups) of sugar, 500 ml (2 cups) of water and 2 halved pods of vanilla into a large pot, heat steadily and stir. Once the butter and sugar melt, add 1/3 of the apples.

Cook for about 10 minutes, so that the apples are at least partly transparent; they shouldn't be cooked fully. Repeat the process with 2/3 of apples and 3/3. Lay the apples on top of the caramel in the mold.

Roll the puff pastry into a rectangle and place it over the apples. Press the edges around the edge of the mold. Pierce with a fork, to create an escape path for the steam. Rub yolk on top.

Bake in an oven preheated to 180°C (350°F) for 30 – 40 minutes, until it turns brown and crunchy. Take out of the oven, let it cool. Flip the mold up side down and remove the cake. Cover with apricot jam, to create a glaze.

APPLE PIE LIKE ROSE BUDS - TARTE AUX POMMES COMME DES BOUTONS DE ROSE

INGREDIENTS:

3 small Golden apples
50 g (¼ cup) butter
biscuits
white chocolate
1 vanilla pods
1 lemon
100 g (1 cup) raspberries
20 g (2 tbsp) raspberry marmalade
rose essence

MAKES 4 SERVINGS

PREPARATION:

Peel the apples. Meanwhile, melt the butter with a pinch of salt. Halve 2 apples, remove the seeds and the cores. Portion the apple on a desk, to get thin (2mm thick) slices. Lay the apples on silicon foil or parchment paper. Lay them in such manner, that they don't overcover fully. At the end rub them with molten butter and sprinkle with sugar. Bake at 210°C (410°F) for 10 minutes.

Crush a handful of white chocolate and melt it in a pan, until it liquefies. Add vanilla and lemon peel. Add crushed biscuits (about 3), shut the flame, take aside and mix once more.

Pour the stuff into a circular mold with a 5cm diameter. Press, until its about 1 cm thick and remove the mold. Shape 3 wheels and place it into the freezer for 5 min., for the dough to thicken.

Cut raspberries in slices and then mix the raspberries with the raspberry jam and add a few drops of the rose essence.

Quarter a whole unpeeled apple. Rub it with lemon as soon as possible, to eliminate oxidation. Cover the quarters with an upside-down glass. It is a part of the serving.

Lay the raspberries with jam on the biscuits with chocolate. Place them with the spoon, such that they would be in the middle of the pastry. Roll the baked apples to create a shape of the rose. Move the rose and lay it on top of the biscuit with the berries. Move the biscuit on top of the upside-down cup.

CARAMEL-GLAZED CREAM PUFFS - CROQUEMBOUCHE

INGREDIENTS:

For the Pâte à Choux
- 12 tbsp unsalted butter
- 1/4 tsp kosher salt
- 2 cups flour
- 9 eggs

To Assemble
- Pastry Cream
- 4 cups sugar

Pastry Cream
- 1 1/2 cups milk
- 1/2 cup sugar
- 3 tbsp cornstarch
- 4 egg yolks
- 1 1/2 tsp vanilla extract
- 16 tbsp butter, softened

MAKES 4 SERVINGS
PREPARATION:

For the pâte à choux: Heat oven to 210°C (425°F). Bring butter, salt, and 1 1/2 cups water to a boil in a 4-qt. saucepan over high heat. Remove pan from heat, add flour all at once, and stir vigorously with a wooden spoon until mixture forms a thick dough and pulls away from sides of pan, about 2 minutes. Return pan to heat and cook, stirring constantly, until dough is lightly dried, about 2 minutes more. Transfer dough to a bowl, and let cool for 5 minutes; using a wooden spoon, beat in 8 eggs, one at a time, making sure each egg is completely incorporated before adding the next. Dough will come together and be thick, shiny, and smooth.

Dip two spoons in water, shake off excess, and scoop a walnut-size piece of dough with one spoon. With other spoon, scrape dough onto parchment-lined baking sheet, setting pieces 1" apart on a baking sheet. Lightly beat remaining egg with pinch of salt and brush each piece of dough with it. Bake until puffed and light brown, about 10 minutes. Reduce oven temperature to 180°C (350°F), and continue to bake until well browned, about 15 minutes. Let cool.

Spoon pastry cream into a pastry bag fitted with a plain 1/4" tip. Gently poke a hole in the flat side of each baked, cooled puff with tip and pipe in filling. For the caramel: Place 2 cups sugar and 1/2 cup water in a shallow saucepan and stir to combine. Cover and cook over medium heat until sugar turns light amber, about 15–20 minutes. Remove from heat.

Using tongs, dip top of filled puffs in hot caramel. Place puffs, glazed side up, on a plastic-lined tray. Form base with 12–14 glazed, cooled puffs, sticking them together with more caramel. Add puffs, layer by layer, to form a hollow cone. (Reheat caramel until liquid again if it becomes too thick; repeat making more caramel with remaining sugar and 1/2 cup water when first batch of caramel becomes too thick to work with.) Allow caramel to cool until it is the consistency

of honey. With a spoon, drizzle thin strings of caramel around cone; let cool until brittle and set. Serve croquembouche within 4 hours of making to ensure the filling doesn't soften the puffs.

Pastry Cream
Bring 1 cup milk and sugar to a boil in a 4-qt. saucepan over medium heat. Meanwhile, whiskr emaining milk, cornstarch, and egg yolks together in a large bowl. Slowly pour half the hot milk into yolk mixture, whisking constantly, then return mixture to saucepan, and cook, stirring constantly with a wooden spoon, until it thickens and just returns to a boil. Stir in vanilla and transfer to a bowl; cover with plastic wrap and refrigerate until chilled. In a large bowl, beat butter on medium speed of a hand mixer until pale and fluffy. Add cold filling and beat until smooth and fluffy, about 4 minutes. Chill until ready to use.

N°10 | FRENCH GASTRONOMY

FROM THE HISTORY OF FRENCH GASTRONOMY

Based on historical and international evaluations, the French cuisine ranks among the leading national cuisines and is at the top of the art of gastronomy. The French cuisine was based on the Italian one, especially from the Roman era, taking basic means of baking and cooking means, as well as the gentleness of the art, from it. Despite the influence of the Italian cuisine, the French one followed its path, reaching its climax in 17th and 18th century. This era is described as the golden age of gastronomy. It is characterized by the economic and industrial growth of France, which reflected on a hedonistic lifestyle of the aristocrats and the bourgeoisie. This created conditions for the development of hospitality and the art of cookery.

Later, the need to restructure the French cuisine emerged, to avoid excessive wasting of resources. The first pioneer of modern French cuisine was Marie-Antoin Careme (1784 – 1833), the master chief of the French emperor, Napoleon I. After his unexpected death, Urbain Dubois took over his work and many incomplete items on the agenda. Dubois and Emil Bernard implemented the second phase. Together, they authored the immortal „La Cuisine Classique" (The Classic Cuisine). They managed to set basic requirements of the art of cookery in this work, the necessary importance of the philosophy of tastes, the delight of the food, the layout and the aesthetics of the meals served. The third phase of the restructuring was led by the trainee of the two masters, Auguste Escoffier (1843 – 1935). Escoffier worked his way up to become the master of the gastronomic art, by his strenuousness and tenacity. He had immense professional knowledge and great taste buds, those allowed him to come up with many new meals and amend old recipes, by regional tendencies. He amended the art of cookery of previous centuries and adapted it to the standards of modern gastronomy. He simplified methods of meal preparation during his career, removing unusable decorative elements, those highlighted the characteristics of individual meals. He had applied simpler means of serving the food and set a firm order of meals when compiling the menus, those he immortalized in his publications: „Guide Culinaire" (The Guide through the culinary) and „Le Livre des Menus" (The Book of Menus).

The 20th century is an era, where the greatest master chefs have emerged. Paul Bocuse, who was chosen as the Chef of the Century and is also the creator of Bocuse d'Or international award, helped to let the vocation of a chef step out of the shadows and he worked to propagate the French cuisine internationally.

Michel Guérard had set the foundations of Nouvelle Cuisine. Other chefs, like the Troisgros brothers, Alain Chapel, George Blanc and others, also became recognized in the era. In late 20th century, there is Alain Ducasse, Guy Savoy, Joël Robuchon, Michel Troisgros, and these are just some of the renowned chefs, who managed to build on their heritage and use the value of local resources.

France is one of the countries, where gastronomy and cookery enjoy great respect and esteem. The French cuisines became famous worldwide, surely also achieved thanks to its massive scale, as all the chefs participated in the progress of gastronomy in the country. Centuries old traditions, natural and climatic conditions, as well as a national character had formed the basis of the globally recognized cuisine. As such thanks to its docility, perfection, smoothness, and application of the contemporary meals of gastronomy, the French cuisine rose over other national cuisines and simultaneously notably influenced the progression of the art of cookery not only in Europe but across the planet.

THE WEALTH OF THE REGIONS

Each region of France is the world in itself and has its own culinary specialties, with those it tries to gain recognition internationally. Good old domestic cuisine or innovative delicacies, light diet or traditional meals, all of that is a part of the gastronomy, which is an inseparable part of French cultural heritage. The tables in fine restaurants surely differ from those across the globe. One thing is constant though and that is the love of the art of cookery, shared by all Frenchman.

French regional cuisines abound many specialties. The natural taste of meat or vegetables is favored and seasoned with herbs (thyme, bay leaves, rosemary or basil) and garnished with parsley leaves or chive.

French cuisine is affected by the cuisines of its former colonies, from where it not only took over the seasonings but also the meals, those have been adapted to fit French tastes. As such African, Chinese or Indian meals are served in restaurants, with their hot and spicy elements omitted.

Each French province has its cuisine and all the regional cuisines combined, enriched with creations of master chefs, created LA CUISINE FRANÇAISE – centered in Paris.

Regional specialties, as masterpieces of ancient cooks, may be found in every region of the land of the Gallic rooster. Every region has its supporters, those write for the press and publicise about the meals available in local pubs and restaurants.

It's fair to say, that the French gastronomy is, as a whole the peak of the art. Most diverse specialties are hence found in French international hotels, as well as smaller restaurants and authentic local pubs. From the cultural and historic view, France is divided into 5 areas. North-western coast (Normandy and Brittany), the east (borderlands with Germany, Switzerland and the Alps), the Mediterranean area (most notably Provence), Southwest of France (borderlands with Spain) and lastly Burgundy and Bordeaux (the most notable wine region of France). The lands around Paris, Ile-de-France, has a special position in French gastronomy, as it is a blend of the previous 5 areas combined.

The best cuisines are in Burgundy, Alsace, Provence, Normandy and, of course, Paris.

THE CUISINE OF BURGUNDY

Its specialty is partridges in an aluminum foil. The partridge is filled with a mix of truffles and wine-steamed goose liver, seasoned with salt and pepper. The opening is sewn together and the partridge is placed into a pork bladder, which is then tied up, immersed into boiling water and cooked for some 30 minutes. The cooked partridge must be cooled and served without any sauce, only with Burgundy red wine.

Another local specialty is the snails. They reach the delicatessen prepared for final preparation. Professionals claim, that they should only be eaten during winter hibernation, from October to March, when the shells are shut with a lime wall.

In Lyon and the nearby regions, a black boudin (a type of sausage) is made. Slices of the sausage are fried with onion on some fat, sprinkled with chopped parsley leaves and dropped with lemon juice. Else the sausages are baked whole (first, each is pierced with a needle, to avoid bursting). Apple puree is served as a side dish.

ALSACE CUISINE

Various famous meat pies are made in from goose liver, in this part of France. There, you can try traditional specialties – saucissons (sausages), choudroute (sauerkraut) and great cheeses. Local gastronomic feasts are very attractive. Even a pork chop with horseradish or baked ham are great meals, going well with wine, but even the beer of Strasbourg is fine.

THE CUISINE OF SOUTHERN FRANCE

The region of Gascony also possesses some specialties. One of them is cassoulet. The famed cassoulet is made with white beans, bacon skin, mutton shoulder, sausage, goose meat pie, goose fat, salt, grounded black pepper, thyme, bay leaves, onion, garlic and white wine.

In the south, a region of Provence spreads around Marseille, where all ingredients yield well, but mainly the olives. If you add fish and garlic to the olive oil, you get the foundation of typical Provence cuisine.

Provence cuisine is simple, although it has notable characteristics and specialties, those have been awarded appropriately. Foreigners, who aren't used to oil and garlic must get used to a different taste of the meals. However, they'll adapt quickly and will soon become the supporters of this healthy cuisine. Garlic may be found in almost every meal. In Provence, on the feast of St. John, the feast of garlic is celebrated as well. Local oil is used as the only fat.

NORTHWESTERN CUISINE

The true cuisine of Normandy is best discovered in the countryside. Rural family tends to dine in the garden. The bowls with the appetizers are laid on the table and the diners pass them along. Every diner has a long piece of white bread – baguette – by their cutlery; it is not sliced, but broken instead. The gourmets claim, that if the baguette is accompanied by cheese and wine, the ‚Holy Trinity' of the French gastronomy is formed.

After the appetizers, an omelet follows (always in a different adaptation) and every diner takes as much as they like. Cheese and fruits are the final courses. In the evening, instead of the appetizers, a soup is served, often followed by a steak. Its aroma and juices must be maintained. Fried potatoes and lettuce are served alongside. Fermented apple drink - cider is often served with the meals. Normandy is famed for its cream, which is used to make the cheese named Camembert. Livestock is grown for meat here. Thin French pancakes (crepes) also originate from Brittany.

Many apple trees are grown in Normandy and Brittany. A juice is fermented from their fruits. It gives a nice, refreshing drink, with low alcohol levels, named cider. It is served along with all types of meat: fish, chickens, livers, Tripes à la mode de Caen – a local specialty. Apples also yield a spirit named calvados. The older pieces tie good cognacs quality wise. These are called calvados hors d'age.

FRENCH CHEESE

France is the symbol of good and quality tastes and unforgettable culinary experiences in the world of gastronomy. This accounts for local cuisines, as well as wines and most diverse delicatessen, which is dominated by cheese.

The diversity of the French production comes from the variations of different regions – each possesses its own methods and recipes, with climatic conditions being an important factor. Normandy is the home to the perhaps most recognized representatives, being home to the Camembert & Brie duo – the soft aromatic cheeses with mold on the surface, those were granted the A.O.P label for the designation of origin (Appellation d'origine protégée – Protected label of origin). Franche-Comté region prides itself with a hard cheese named Comté, made from the fat milk of cows grown in the pastures of the Jura Mountains. Goat cheeses are also widely represented in France – declared varieties are made in the valley of Loire or in the region of Poitou-Charentes. Cheeses of sheep milk are the domain of mountainous areas – Roquefort, a soft cheese with blue mold on the surface, originates from the regions of mid-Pyrenees and is now renowned across the globe. It is said that there are more cheese types in France, than there are days in a year – hence the lovers of the delicacy have plenty to explore.

THE NOBLE BLUE

Cheeses with blue mold are some of the discoveries of French gastronomy and their production steadily spread to the rest of the world. The unique taste and structure are attributed to the noble mold, Penicillium Roqueforti, which is natural to some caves in the mountains. It initially got to the cheese through the air and then spread through the structures of the cheese.

Contemporary cheese production applies the mold directly to the curd and the cheese is pierced during the process, so as to support the growth of the cultures. Roquefort is one of the most famous representatives of sheep milk cheeses, even today maturing in the caves. Bleu d'Auvergne also maintains a notable name, which is made from cow milk. The taste, aroma, and consistency of the cheeses with blue mold depends on the level of maturity – the younger types are softer and crumbly, mature once have a bolder taste and a more compact structure.

VAL DE LOIRE & POITOU CHARENTES
HOW IS GOAT CHEESE MADE?
All French cheeses of the goat milk are known as „chevre" („chevre" = goat). „Mi-chevre" cheeses are made from goat and cow milk, mixed in 50/50 ratio. After a goat gives birth to the baby,

it gives milk for about 9 months (about 4 liters per day = 800 liters per year; 100 l of milk can make about 11 kg of cheese). Unpasteurized milk is precipitated at 33 °C after filtration. The resultant mass is placed into the mould with openings on the bottom, or alternatively might be packed with herbs or vine leaves. After the whey drops away, the cheese is removed from the molds and dries for 3 days at open air and matures for at least 20 days in a cold and wet cellar. The longer, the harder and drier the cheese will be and they will have a bolder taste. It is said that the cheeses from the milk made in May and June are the best, as the pastures are full of fresh grass.

Goat cheeses are right mainly for the cold cuisine. They are best with fresh fruits (grapes, figs, cranberries), walnuts, honey or marmalade.

They may be grilled lightly as a whole, or individually in pieces, wrapped in English bacon. They are also utilizable in salty rolls, pizzas, baking and in salad making.

EMMENTAL
A cheese of a unique look and taste originates from Switzerland, but even in France it has a lasting tradition – Emmental de Savoie

and Emmental Français Est-Central Grand Cru I.G.P., from the Franche-Comté region, even prides itself on a label of protected origin. Emmental is classified as a hard cheese, but it stands out from the rest by a view of the dough. It is made from pasteurized or raw cow milk, which is enriched with yeast after precipitating.

Styling, pressing and salt bath follows, leading to a phase of maturing in cooling chambers. During the time fermentation process endures and causes the creation of carbon dioxide and characteristic holes in the dough. Younger Emmental has a slightly sweeter taste, while the mature units tend to be richer in the walnut tones and a long maturing cheese might be slightly spicy and hot.

EMMENTAL IN THE KITCHEN
Emmental has a wide scale of application in hot and cold cuisine. It melts easily, making it a right ingredient for fondue or baked meat, vegetable or pasta dishes. It goes well with potatoes and is fit for sandwiches, salads and might even stand alone as a dessert cheese, to be served with wine.

BRIE
Brie is a soft cheese with surface mold. It originated from the French department of Seine-et-Marne, but its contemporary successors are Brie de Meaux and Brie de Melun. Brie de Meaux is sold in the shape of flat circular loafs, weighing 908 – 3,200 grams. Its white crusts with pink/beige marbling diversify it from many fake imitations. The dough has a shiny straw-colored shade, which deepens to a warm ivory color. Mature cheese may grow, but it doesn't flow out. It might have a cellar aroma or the aroma of fried nuts and sometimes even a slight stink of ammonia. The taste is very complex with nut and even fruity flavors. Brie de Melun is slightly smaller and matures longer than Brie de Meaux. It has a very dark grid crust, with only occasional hints of white. The dough is of golden yellow color. The aroma and the taste are more dominant and rustic than in the case of Brie de Meaux. The traditional Brie may be made from pasteurized and unpasteurized milk. The curd is not cut or pressed. The art is in the laying the layers of curd to the molds and removing the whey. Moulded cheeses are deposited to straw mats and turn regularly. After a week, they are sprayed with penicillin mold and are left to mature at a set temperature, until done.

TWO VARIATIONS OF RACLETTE
Just as many delicacies, raclette came about by accident – a melter from the Swiss Alps apparently tripped over and fell, while the cheese he held in his hand fell into the fire. He quickly removed it from the fire and rubbed the semi-molten part on to a bread, giving birth to a tradition named by the verb raclette,

to scrub. The name however only emerged in 1909, when local poet Perollaz first used it to describe the meal and the cheese. This, however, didn't stop the disputes between France and Switzerland, regarding the origin. Consequently, both countries hold the protective label – in case of Swiss Raclette Valais it is the A.O.P – Appellation d'origine protégée (Label of protected origin), while French Raclette de Savoie carries I.G.P. label (Indication géographique protégée – Indication of protected geography). Swiss Raclette is somewhat bigger and thicker, matures longer (at least 3 months, 5 – 6 months is the desired period) and is characteristic thanks to its spicier taste. Also available in the angular shape, commonly seasoned with black pepper, capsicum, garlic or by smoking it. French producers

tune the taste towards a noble cream taste and aroma. It also varies by the way of serving the same meal – in French restaurants, each table utilizes a small electric grill alone and serves themselves, while in Switzerland a professional usually walks through the restaurant, scraping the cheese on to the potatoes himself. Both countries tend to serve light dry wines with bold acidity. In Switzerland, it's mainly the local Fendant wine, made of the Chasselas grapes.

FRENCH DINING

The style of French dining reaps admiration and fame worldwide. It is grandiose, noble but it keeps its comfortability. Locals are proud of it, since it's an integral part of their culture, their personality. The French simply hold fashionable dining as important.

The French dining truly deserves a special mention. An average Frenchmen spends more than an hour at the lunch or dinner table on a normal day, which may extend up to 4 – 5 hours on Sundays or feasts! In a way, it is the right thing to do, as the meals are consumed slowly, a slow and natural conversation flows and creates a welcoming atmosphere. It is rude to visit someone, without their declared invitation, in France. This, however is comprehendible, as the Madame of the household tends to prepare a complete lunch or dinner for the occasion, hence the fate of all the dinners is her responsibility.

Going to a restaurant can be described as a natural hobby. The French love to meet and enjoy a good meal or a drink together, to get away from the business of the common day and to get to talk about the joys or worries they might have. No one rushes anywhere, all consider a shared meal to be a social event. The French don't eat just to meet their needs, but also to spend time with a pleasant company, to enjoy the given moment and to have a chat.

French style of dining is very pleasant. Eating is considered a social event, there is a lot of talking and no one rushes. At least one hour is reserved for lunch, even if it is a lunch at work. Dinner is thought of as the most important part of the day, commencing at 8pm at earliest and being a place for the entire family to meet. In France, dining became a ritual. At all times, the lunch/dinner is of a few smaller courses, usually five. A jug of water or wine can't be absent, neither can be the bread and butter. The day begins with the breakfast, those, however, aren't that important. The French sit at the table at mid-day and in the evening. In France, every dining consists of multiple courses. First the aperitif is served, followed by the appetizers. Then the main course follows, topped by a delicious dessert. Sometimes, however, a special fourth course may be encountered, which consists only of cheese. It usually precedes the dessert.

A baguette is served with all the courses (except for the sweet desserts, of course) and pieces of it are broken over the table, not over the plate. Other, traditional side dishes aren't eaten in mass by the French. This includes rice or pasta. These are common in the canteens. It is interesting, that all the courses (except for the dessert), are served in the same type of plate.

This custom is observed in restaurants, just as at home.

The French breakfasts tend to be sweet and mostly simple. Very soft croissants, chocolate breads (pain au chocolat) and varied sweet pastries, those we probably couldn't find in any other country, are enjoyed in the morning.

The French like to eat various types of meat or fish for lunch, with the side dish of steamed vegetables, popular baguettes or plain potatoes. Leaves of a salad are an important article in the diet. Multiple of these are offered by the restaurants, nicely and neatly torn, and laid through the plate. Apparently, they are eaten to lower the cholesterol levels in the blood stream.

It is common, if the dessert consists of three courses. A cheese platter, fruits and cakes are followed in a specific order. The portions don't have to be large, on the contrary they're quite symbolic. Even a yoghurt may pass a sufficient dessert. French yoghurts may appear quite strange at the first sight, usually white, perhaps with a fruity flavour and the consistency of a jelly.

The dinner is the most important course of the day. It's served at 8pm and usually an entire family assembles for it. Instead of an appetizer, a soup dominates, but when visiting a fine restaurant, fabled delicacies, such as snail, juicy mussels or oysters are a popular choice. The French dine for a long time and take pleasure in doing so, not letting a single piece of the food go to waste. They even frequently wipe the plate with a baguette or a piece of white bread.

If you want to visit a luxurious restaurant, don't forget to book your table. The main course is ordered first, a selection from the wine list is made later. The choice of a quality wine may be crucial.

France indeed offers many gourmet attractions and benefits. Dining in the country is of a high quality and is approached with elegance.

Enjoying an evening in luxurious restaurant of France, with a nice company, is simply an indescribable experience, but even you may enjoy it during your business or a family trip to Paris, or other spots across France.

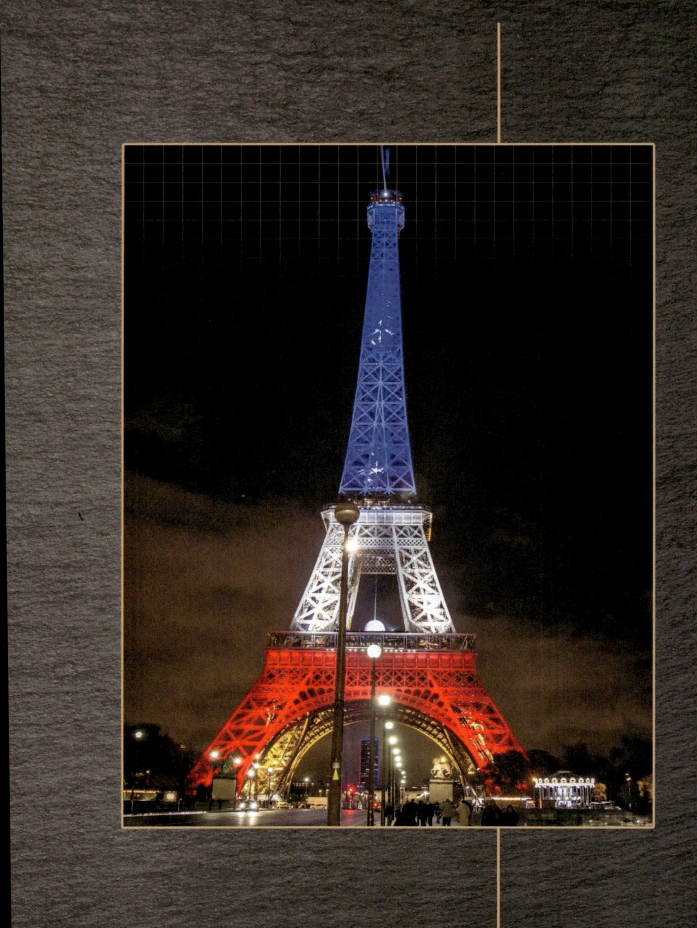

Printed in Great Britain
by Amazon